AF527051

فضائلِ رمضان

Faza'il - E - Ramazan

Virtues of Ramadhan

Moulana Muhammad Zakariyyah Kandehlawi

Qadeem PRESS

Virtues of Ramadhaan

Written By: Sheikhul Hadeeth, Hadhrat Moulana Muhammad Zakariyya رَحْمَةُ اللهِ عَلَيْه

Published by: Ta'limi Board (KZN)
4 Third Avenue
P.O.Box 26024
Isipingo Beach
4115
South Africa

Tel: +27-31 912 2172
Fax: +27-31 902 9268
E-mail: info@talimiboardkzn.org
Website: www.talimiboardkzn.org

First edition: September 2007
Second edition: May 2011

- For the *esaale thawaab* of the entire *Ummah* of Nabi ﷺ.
- Open permission is granted for reprinting of this booklet provided it is without any alterations.
- A humble appeal is directed to readers to offer suggestions, corrections, etc. to improve the quality of this publication in the future. May Allah ﷻ reward you for this.
- The author, translators, editors, sponsors and typesetters humbly request your *duas* for them, their parents, families, *Mashaaikh* and *Asaatidha*.

Contents

Ramadhaan, the month of Rewards

Rasulullah ﷺ Lecture on the last day of Shabaan

Salmaan رضي الله عنه says that on the last day of Shabaan, Rasulullah ﷺ spoke us and said:

"O People, there comes to you a great month now, a most blessed month, in which is a night greater in value and goodness than a thousand months. It is a month in which Allah ﷻ has made fasting fardh by day and has made *sunnah* the *Taraweeh Salaah* by night. Whosoever wants to be close to Allah ﷻ by doing any good deed, for such person shall be the reward like the one who had performed a *fardh* in any other time and whoever performs a *fardh*, shall be given the reward of **seventy** *faraaidh* in any other time."

This is indeed the month of patience and the reward for true patience is *Jannah* (paradise). It is the month of showing kindness to everyone. It is the month in which a true believer's *rizq* (food, money, etc.) are increased. Whosoever feeds a fasting person in order to break the fast at *iftaar* (sunset), for him there shall be forgiveness of sins and freedom from the fire of *Jahannam* (hell) and he shall receive the same reward as the fasting person (whom he fed) without the fasting person losing any reward.

Thereupon we said, 'O Messenger of Allah ﷺ, not all of us can afford to give a fasting person something to break his fast with.' Rasulullah ﷺ replied, 'Allah ﷻ gives the same reward to the one who gives a fasting person to break the fast, just one date or a drink of water or a sip of milk.'

This is a month, the first of which brings Allah's ﷻ mercy, the middle of which brings His forgiveness and the last of which brings freedom from the fire of *Jahannam.*

Whosoever gives less work to his servants or workers (who are also fasting in this month), Allah ﷻ will forgive him and free him from the fire of *Jahannam.*

In this month four things you should perform in great number, two of which shall be to please Allah ﷻ, while the other two shall be those which you cannot do without. Those which shall be to please Allah ﷻ, are that you should recite in great number the *Kalimah Tayibbah - Laa ilaaha illallah* (i.e. To bear witness that there is no god except Allah ﷻ) and to recite *istighfaar* (beg Allah's ﷻ forgiveness with *astaghfirullah*) and as for those which you cannot do without, you should beg of Allah ﷻ for entrance into *Jannah* and ask protection in Him from *Jahannam.*

And whoever gives a fasting person water to drink, Allah ﷻ shall grant him to drink from my fountain, such a drink, after which that person shall never feel thirsty again until he enters *Jannah.*" (Reported by Ibn Khuzaimah in his 'Saheeh'.)

Commentry:

All the points in this *Hadeeth* have been explained in many other *Ahaadeeth* on the great rewards of Ramadhaan.

Rasulullah ﷺ gave this lecture at the end of Shabaan, because he wanted to show us the great importance of Ramadhaan so that we do not allow one second of this month to go to waste.

Fasting has been made fardh by Allah ﷻ who has also made sunnah the *Taraweeh Salaah* by night.

From this *Hadeeth* we learn that the command for *Taraweeh Salaah* too comes from Allah ﷻ Himself. Besides this, in all the *Ahaadeeth* where Rasulullah ﷺ says, I have made it ***Sunnah*** is to stress its importance. All the *Ulama'* are agreed upon the fact that *Taraweeh* is *Sunnah.* Moulana Shah Abdullah Dehlawi in his book, '*Maa Thabata Bis Sunnah*', states that if the people of any town do not perform *Taraweeh Salaah*, the Muslim ruler should make them do so by force.

Many people say that you may listen to the full Qur'aan being read in a certain *Musjid* in eight or ten nights and then stop performing *Taraweeh* with *jamaat* as the *sunnah* will have been fulfilled. This is wrong, by doing this only one *sunnah* will be fulfilled and the other lost. We should remember that there are two separate *sunnats*. Firstly, it is *sunnah* to hear the full Qur'aan being read in the *Taraweeh* in Ramadhaan. Secondly, it is *sunnah* to perform *Taraweeh* with *jamaat* for men in the *Musjid* throughout Ramadhaan. Females should perform their *Taraweeh* at home.

Another point that we learn in the *Hadeeth* is that Rasulullah ﷺ told us that any *nafil* done in Ramadhaan is rewarded as much as a *fardh* in normal times and a *fardh* done in Ramadhaan has the reward of seventy *fardh* at other times.

Our Faults

Is our *ibaadah* or worship in Ramadhaan important to us? How many *nafil* do we perform? We see how many people, who after having eaten *sehri*, go back to bed without performing the *Fajr Salaah*. Many perform it, but not with *jamaat*. Someone might think that we give thanks to Allah ﷻ for the food we had eaten for *sehri* by not performing the most important *fardh* or by not performing it with *jamaat.* Such a *Salaah* is not complete.

Rasulullah ﷺ said: "There is no *Salaah* for those near the *Musjid* except in the *Musjid.*" In the *kitaab 'Mazhaahir-e-Haq'* we find that there is no reward for *Salaah,* for people who do not perform it with *jamaat,* without any good reason or excuse.

Similarly, in many cases at the time of *iftaar, Maghrib Salaah* is missed and many do not come to the *Musjid.* Some miss the *takbeer* at the beginning or miss the first *rakaat.* Many people hurry to get over the *Taraweeh Salaah* and even perform the *Esha Salaah* before the time of *Esha* starts. (Some do not pay any attention to *Salaah* even in Ramadhaan).

That is the condition of our *fardh Salaah* in Ramadhaan. Whilst performing one *fardh* of fasting, three others are destroyed. How often do we see that even the time of *Zuhr Salaah* passes by because we are asleep, while the time of *Asr* goes by because we are too busy buying, selling or cooking to prepare for *iftaar.*

If such is the case with the *faraaidh,* then we can imagine how much less importance is given to the *nafil* actions. One finds that because of sleep, the times of *Salaatul Ishraaq* (after sunrise) and *Salaatud Dhuhaa* (before noon) go by.

Then what about *Salaatul Awwabeen* (just after *Maghrib*)? Here we find ourselves busy with *iftaar* and when thinking about *Taraweeh* after *Esha* this *Salaah* too is neglected. Further we find that for *Salaatut Tahajjud* the time is the same as that for *sehri* with the result that this too goes by. One may make a thousand excuses for not finding time for these *nawaafil.* These are all excuses for not performing these *Salaah.*

Advice

There is very strong link between Ramadhaan and the *Tilaawat* of the Qur'aan. Almost all Allah ﷻ great holy books were sent down in this month. Similarly, in this month the Qur'aan was brought down from the *'lowhul mahfoozh'* (preserved tablet) to the *'samaaud dunyaa'* (Earthly sky), from where it was revealed bit by bit to Rasulullah ﷺ in a period of twenty three years.

There is a great connection between the Qur'aan and the month of Ramadhaan. For this reason, as much *Tilaawat* of the Qur'aan as possible should be made during this month. Such was the habit of our pious people of the past. Jibraeel عليه السلام used to recite the whole Qur'aan to our Nabi ﷺ in the month of Ramadhaan. In some reports it is stated that Rasulullah ﷺ used to recite and Jibraeel عليه السلام used to listen.

The *Ulama'* have said that it is Mustahab to read Qur'aan in such a manner that while one recites the other listens. Thereafter, another recites while others listen. So recite the Qur'aan as much as possible. Whatever time remains thereafter should not be wasted.

Rasulullah ﷺ drew our attention to four things and advised that we should practice them as much as possible. They are the recitation of ***Kalimah Tayibbah, istighfaar, begging for Jannah and asking safety from Jahannam.*** Therefore, it must be regarded an honour to spend as much time as possible reciting these. This will be the true appreciation of the teachings of Rasulullah ﷺ. What is so difficult about keeping the tongue busy with the recitation of *Durood* (*salawaat*) or *'Laa Ilaha illallah'* while being engaged in our daily works?

In the same *Hadeeth*, Rasulullah ﷺ said a few more things; Ramadhaan is the month of patience. So if great difficulty is experienced in fasting, one should bear it with patience. One should not complain as people are fond of doing during hot days. If by chance *sehri* is missed then too one should not complain. Similarly, should any difficulty or trial be experienced, one should bear it with patience; otherwise, these deeds may possibly be empty of *barakah* (blessings). When we avoid the worldly pleasures and give up our eating and drinking, then for the sake of Allah's ﷻ pleasure what are these difficulties.

Kindness for the poor & unfortunate

The *Hadeeth* also says that it is the month of sympathy and kindness, especially for the poor and needy. Sympathy should be of a practical nature. When ten things are placed before us for *iftaar*, at least two or four of them should be set aside for the poor and needy. They should be treated more favourably, if not then at least equally and should certainly be remembered. The *Sahaabah* ؓ were living examples in showing sympathy for the poor, it is our duty to follow or at least try to follow them.

In the matter of sacrifice and sympathy, only the brave can follow the examples of *Sahaabah* ؓ. There are many instances which will leave one in amazement if mentioned.

Let us see the following example, Abu Jahm ؓ relates that, during the battle of Yarmouk, he went in search of his cousin, taking with him a water bag to give him to drink and also wash his wounds if he was found alive or wounded. He found him lying among the wounded. When I asked him whether he wanted some water, he said 'Yes'. At that moment someone near him moaned. My cousin pointed to that person indicating that I should first give him the water. I went to him and found that he too needed water, but just as I was about to give him the water, a third person groaned near him. The second one pointed to this third person meaning that I should give the third one to drink first. I went to the third person but before he could drink, I found out that he had passed away, I then returned to the second one only to find that he too had passed away. When I came back to my cousin, he too had become a *shaheed.*

This is the type of caring character our *Sahaabah* ؓ had. They preferred to die thirsty rather than to drink before a Muslim brother.

May Allah ﷻ be pleased with them all and grant us ability to follow in their footsteps. *Aameen*

Another *Hadeeth* says that whoever feeds the hungry, clothes the naked and gives shelter to the traveller, Allah ﷻ shall save him from the terrors of *Qiyaamah.* Further, Rasulullah ﷺ mentioned the virtue of feeding a fasting person at the time of breaking the fast. In one *Hadeeth* it is reported that one who feeds a person out of his *Halaal* earnings to break the fast, the *Malaaikah* grant mercy upon him during the nights of Ramadhaan, and Jibraeel ﷺ shakes hands with him on *Laylatul Qadr.* The sign of this is that his heart becomes soft and tears flow from his eyes.

During Ramadhaan, Hammad bin Salamah, a very famous *Muhaddith,* used to feed fifty people every day at *iftaar. (Roohul Bayan)*

Thereafter, the *Hadeeth* of Rasulullah ﷺ called the first section (i.e. first 10 days) of Ramadhaan the coming of mercy, which means that Allah's ﷻ favour is with the believers. Those who are thankful to Allah ﷻ for His bounties will receive even more. The Qur'aan says:

"If you are thankful, I will surely grant you more."

During the second section (i.e. the second 10 days) of Ramadhaan, forgiveness begins to come down as a reward for fasting during the first section. The last section (i.e. the last 10 days) of Ramadhaan brings protection from entrance into *Jahannam.* This is supported by many similar *Ahaadeeth.*

In my personal opinion, Ramadhaan has been divided into three sections because people are normally of three different kinds. Firstly, there are those who have no sins. For them Allah's mercy and Bounties come from the very beginning of Ramadhaan. Secondly, there are those whose sins are not too heavy, for them forgiveness comes after one third of Ramadhaan has passed. Thirdly, there are the real sinners. For them forgiveness comes after having fasted most of Ramadhaan. Those who received Allah ﷻ mercy right at the beginning are the very fortunate ones because of the great amount of mercy they have received. (And Allah ﷻ knows best).

Another point mentioned in the *Ahaadeeth* is that masters should be merciful to their servants in Ramadhaan because, after all, they too are fasting. Unnecessary hard work or too much of it will be difficult for them. An extra worker should be hired when the work is too much. That of course, only applies when the servant himself fasts; otherwise there is no difference for them between Ramadhaan and any other month.

Lastly, Rasulullah ﷺ encouraged four things in the *Hadeeth* that should be repeated constantly. Firstly, the recitation of *Kalimah Tayyibah*, which in the *Ahaadeeth* is called the highest form of *zikr*. In Mishkat, Abu Saeed Khudri رضي الله عنه reports: Once Nabi Moosa عليه السلام begged of Allah ﷻ to grant him a special *zikr* by which he can remember Allah ﷻ and also (by which he could) ask Him. Allah ﷻ then told him to recite the *Kalimah Tayyibah*. Sayyidina Moosa عليه السلام said, "O Allah! this is a *zikr* recited by all your servants, I wish for a special *zikr*." Allah ﷻ replied, "O Moosa, if the seven heavens, the earth and all its occupants including the *Malaaikah* but excluding Myself (i.e. excluding Allah ﷻ Himself) are placed on one side of a scale and this *Kalimah* on the other, then this *Kalimah* will weigh heavier than everything else.

In another *Hadeeth* it is stated, Should anyone sincerely recite this *Kalimah*, the doors of *Jannah* open up for him immediately and nothing can stop him from reaching Allah ﷻ *arsh* (throne). The only condition is that the reciter should stay away from major sins.

The *Kalimah Tayyibah* is the most excellent form of *zikr*. Allah ﷻ has made it for everybody, so that none is deprived of it. Therefore, if any person is deprived of it, it is his own fault. There are many *Ahaadeeth* showing its rewards.

The second thing which should be recited plentifully is *istighfaar*. The *Ahaadeeth* report many rewards of *istighfaar*. In one *Hadeeth* we read, "Whoever makes much *Istighfaar*, Allah ﷻ opens a way out for him from all problems and removes all sadness from him. He also receives *rizq* (food, money etc.) from unexpected places." In another *Hadeeth*, Rasulullah ﷺ said that, "Every man is a sinner, but the best among the sinners are those who repent and ask for forgiveness." In one *Hadeeth* it is mentioned that, "When a man commits a sin, a black spot forms on his heart, but when he asks for forgiveness, it is washed away , if not, the black spot remains".

Thereafter, Rasulullah ﷺ commanded us to beg two things which we cannot do without, firstly to beg Allah ﷻ for entrance into *Jannah* and secondly to ask for protection in Him from *Jahannam*.

May Allah ﷻ grant us this good fortune. (*Aameen*)

Five Gifts given to this Ummah in Ramadhaan

Abu Hurairah رضي الله عنه says that Rasulullah ﷺ said, "My *ummah* has been given five special things that were not given to anyone before them. The smell from the mouth of a fasting Muslim is sweeter for Allah ﷻ than the sweet smell of musk. The fish in the sea ask for forgiveness for them until they break their fast. Allah ﷻ prepares and decorates His special *Jannah* every day and then says: "The time is near when My loyal servants shall put away the load (of the world) and come to you." The evil *shayateen* are chained in this month of Ramadhaan so as not to take people towards evils which they normally do during other months. On the last night of Ramadhaan, the fasting Muslims are forgiven. The *Sahaabah* رضي الله عنهم then asked, "O Rasulullah ﷺ, is that the night of *Laylatul Qadr*?" Rasulullah ﷺ replied, "No, But it is only right that a servant should be given his reward on having completed his duty."

Note: These five gifts from Allah ﷻ were not granted to the (fasting) people before Islam. If only we could truly appreciate how great this gift from Allah ﷻ really is, we will sincerely try to get these special favours.

First, we are told that the smell from the mouth of the fasting person is more pleasing to Allah ﷻ than the smell of musk. There are three most acceptable explanations:

a) Some say that, in the *Aakhirah* (Hereafter), Allah ﷻ shall reward that smell from the mouth with a pleasing smell more sweet and refreshing than musk. *(Durre Manthur)*
b) On the day of *Qiyamah* when we shall rise from our graves, a sweet smell shall come from the mouths of those who fasted and that shall be better than musk.
c) In my opinion, the view that in this very world the smell is more pleasing for Allah ﷻ than musk. This shows the ties of love between Allah ﷻ and His fasting slaves.

We all know that even a bad smell from a person, whom one loves truly and sincerely, is in itself attractive to the lover, who in this case is Allah ﷻ Himself. What is shown is how close to Allah ﷻ a fasting person is.

Fasting is one of the most pleasing forms of worship in the sight of Allah ﷻ and for this reason a *Hadeeth* states that for every deed the reward is brought by the *Malaaikah*, but Allah ﷻ says, "The reward for fasting, I Myself will give, because it is for Me alone". Another report of the same *Hadeeth* (when read in a different way) says "I Myself become his reward". And what greater reward can there be for the lover than to meet the Beloved?

In another *Hadeeth* we read, "Fasting is the door to all other forms of worship of Allah ﷻ". This means that, through fasting, the heart becomes encouraged to other forms of worship. This is the case if the fast is kept properly (as shall be explained later), and is not merely remaining hungry and thirsty.

The second special favour is that the fish in the sea ask for forgiveness for the person who fasts. The purpose here is to explain that many living things make *dua* for him. My uncle, Moulana Muhammad Ilyas رَحْمَةُ اللهِ عَلَيْهِ used to say that this is so because Allah ﷻ says in the Holy Qur'aan, "Certainly those who believe and do righteous deeds, Allah ﷻ shall make them beloved (in this world)" *(Surah Maryam 96)*

One *Hadeeth* explains this further, "When Allah ﷻ loves a person, He says to the angel Jibraeel عليه السلام, 'I love that person, so you also love him.' Jibraeel عليه السلام then also loves that person and announces in the first heaven that, 'That person is loved by Allah ﷻ, you all should also love him.' Then all the creations of the heavens begin to love him. Then, love for that person spreads all over the earth." Normally only those who are near to a person seem to love him, but here that love spreads all over, even the animals in the jungle and the fish in the sea do the same. They all then make *dua* on his behalf.

The third favour given to the fasting persons is that *Jannah* is decorated for them. The *Hadeeth* states that at the beginning of every year, *Jannah* begins to be decorated for Ramadhaan. We know that when an important person is expected to arrive, great care is taken in the preparations for his welcome. For example, in a marriage preparations start months in advance, likewise it is with Ramadhaan.

The fourth favour is that evil *shayateen* (devils) are chained, so evil is much less. One would have expected that, because of the great desire for worship of Allah ﷻ in the blessed month of Ramadhaan, the *shayateen* would try just as hard to pull the faithful away from the right path, so that much more evil would be committed. That is not the case. Instead we see so much less evil. How many drunkards do we see, who just because of the blessed month of Ramadhaan, do not drink any wine? How many other sinners we see giving up evil acts during the blessed month of Ramadhaan?

You may wonder that, when the *shayateen* are chained, how is it that we still see sins being committed, even though in lesser amounts? The reply is that all evil may not necessarily be caused by the evil *shayateen.* Having for eleven months lived in obedience to the wishes of the *shayateen,* the doing of evil actions caused by them becomes a habit and so evil is being done in Ramadhaan and also out of Ramadhaan. For this reason we find those who normally commit sins continue to do some of it in Ramadhaan. Thus, even though *shayateen* have been chained, their effect on us has become so strong that we follow their ways from our own side even in Ramadhaan.

Another important point is that Nabi ﷺ has said, "When a person commits a sin, a black spot forms on his heart, when he sincerely makes *taubah* (repents), it is removed otherwise it remains. When he again commits a sin another spot forms (and so on), until his heart becomes completely black. Then nothing good can enter his heart."

Referring to this, Allah ﷻ says in the Qur'aan, *"Never! But on their heart is the stain (of Evil)" (Al-Munafiqeen 14).* Thus their hearts become totally stained, in such cases, these hearts are obviously attracted towards sins. This is the reason why many people without any fear do one type of sin, but when thinking of another similar sin, then their hearts refuse to do it.

For example, if those people who drink wine are told to eat pork, they would hate it, whereas these two evils are equally sinful. Similarly, the heart is stained by them, thus resulting in these sins being done even without any action of the *shayateen.*

My personal opinion is that not all the *shayateen* are chained, but only the most evil ones. All of us can see that in Ramadhaan, It does not require a great amount of effort and energy to perform a good act. Neither does it need a great amount of self control and effort to avoid sin, as in other times.

Moulana Shah Ishaaq was of the opinion that, for the evil people, only the most evil *shayateen* are chained, whereas for the pious ones all *shayateen* are chained.

The fifth favour is that forgiveness is granted on the last night of Ramadhaan. (See previous *Hadeeth*). Because of this great favour, the *Sahaabah* ﷺ thought that this night must be *Laylatul Qadr.* They knew the great blessings of that night and asked whether it meant *Laylatul Qadr.* The reply was that it was not. This is just a favour granted for having fasted to the end of Ramadhaan.

Only a Very Unfortunate Person would not get forgiveness in Ramadhaan

Kaab Ibn Ujrah ﷺ says that Rasulullah ﷺ said, "Come near to the *mimbar*" and we came near the *mimbar.* When He climbed the first step of the mimbar, He said "*Aameen*", When He climbed the second step, He said "*Aameen*", When He climbed the third step, He said "*Aameen*" When He came down, We said "O Rasul of Allah ﷺ, today we have heard from you something which we had never heard before." Rasulullah ﷺ said, "When I climbed the first step, Jibraeel ﷺ appeared before me and said, "Destruction to the person who found the blessed month of Ramadhaan and let it pass by without gaining forgiveness," then, I said '*Aameen.*' When I climbed the second step, he said, "Destruction to the person before whom your (i.e. Nabi's ﷺ) name is taken and he does not send *Durood* and Salaam on you (for example by saying, *Sallallahu Alayhi Wasallam*)." I replied '*Aameen.*' When I climbed the third step, he said "Destruction on that person in whose lifetime both his parents or either one of them reaches old age, and (because of not serving them) he is not allowed to enter *Jannah.*" I said '*Aameen.*'

Note: In this Hadeeth, Jibraeel عليه السلام made three curses, upon which Rasulullah ﷺ said "*Aameen*" every time.

In al-Durr al-Mansoor, it is said that Jibraeel عليه السلام asked Rasulullah ﷺ to say '*Aameen*'. The curses of Jibraeel عليه السلام, an angel of such high position, are sure to be accepted. May Allah ﷻ in His mercy grant us His help and save us from these three curses.

The first person described above is he who, even in the blessed month of Ramadhaan, spends the days in sin and does not worry about his duties, thus he does not get forgiveness. Ramadhaan is the month of Allah's ﷻ mercy and if even this month is spent carelessly, how can he expect to be forgiven for his sins? If he cannot gain Allah's ﷻ forgiveness in Ramadhaan, then when will he do so? The way to seek Allah's ﷻ pardon for his sins is to complete his duties in Ramadhaan as ordered by Allah ﷻ, such as fasting, reading *Taraweeh Salaah* and asking for Allah's ﷻ forgiveness for past sins.

The second unfortunate person is he who hears the name of Rasulullah's ﷺ and yet does not send *Durood* and *Salaam* on him. For this reason, some *Ulama'* consider it compulsory to recite *Durood* whenever the name of Muhammad ﷺ is mentioned. In some *Ahaadeeth*, the person who fails to do so is called unfortunate and stingy. Such people are described as those who would lose the way to Jannah, or even among those who will enter Jahannam or those who will not look upon the blessed face of Rasulullah ﷺ. The Ulama give us many meanings to these *Ahaadeeth*. Not sending *Durood* and *Salaam* on Nabi ﷺ is very unfortunate.

Why should it not be? After all, the favours on us because of Rasulullah ﷺ are so great that our writings and our lectures cannot describe. His favours on us are very great. Therefore, any warning, for the neglect of sending *Durood* and *Salaam* on Nabi ﷺ, is acceptable.

On the other hand, the reward for reciting *Durood* is very great. The *Hadeeth* teaches us that whosoever recites *Durood* once, Allah ﷻ sends ten blessings on him and the *Malaaikah* make *dua* for him. All his sins are forgiven, his position is raised and his reward will be as big as mount Uhud and on the day of *Qiyamah*, Rasulullah ﷺ shall ask Allah ﷻ to forgive him.

More promises of reward are: obtaining Allah's ﷻ happiness, mercy and safety against His anger, safety from the fears of *Qiyamah*, seeing your place in *Jannah* while still alive on this earth. Besides these, there is the promise of never being troubled by poverty and of enjoying nearness to Rasulullah ﷺ, the promise of help against enemies and the promise of being loved by others. It is compulsory to recite *Durood* at least once in a lifetime and all the *Ulama'* are agreed upon this fact. However, some *Ulama' say that Durood* must be recited whenever the name of Rasulullah ﷺ is mentioned while others say it is preferable.

The third person described in the *Hadeeth* above, is he in whose lifetime one or both of his parents reach old age, and yet he is unable to gain *Jannah* by serving them. The *Ulama'* have stated that in every permissible act, it is compulsory to obey the parents' commands. You should not be disrespectful to them and you should be be humble, even though they may be non muslims. You must neither raise your voice above theirs, nor call them by their names. When they have to be called towards good and stopprd from evil, it should be done mercifully and you should continue to make *dua* for them even if they refuse to accept.

In a *Hadeeth* it is said that, at all times they should be honoured and respected. It is also related that the best of doors for entering *Jannah* is the father. If you wish, look after it and if you wish, destroy it.

A *Sahaabi* رضي الله عنه asked Rasulullah ﷺ, "What are the rights due to parents?" He ﷺ replied, "They are your *Jannah* and your *Jahannam*! I.e. if they are happy, it leads you to *Jannah* while their unhappiness leads you to *Jahannam*." It is stated in a *Hadeeth* that when an obedient son looks with love and affection at his parents, the reward for that look shall be an accepted Hajj. In another *Hadeeth*, it is stated that Allah ﷻ forgives all sins as He pleases except the sin of *shirk* (i.e. joining partners with Allah ﷻ). However, He causes punishment for disobedience to parents, right in this world before death.

A *Sahaabi* ؓ said, "O Rasul of Allah ﷺ, I want to go for *Jihad*." Rasulullah ﷺ asked, "Is your mother alive?" "Yes," He replied. Rasulullah ﷺ then said, "Serve her, *Jannah* lies under her feet". Again another *Hadeeth* says, "The pleasure of Allah ﷻ is in pleasing your father, and Allah's ﷻ displeasure is in displeasing your father."

However, if ones parents were not respected and treated properly and have passed away, there is still something that their children can do according to Islam. The *Hadeeth* teaches us that, in such cases, one should always make *dua* for their forgiveness. By doing so, you will be counted among those who are obedient. Another *Hadeeth* says that the best action a person can do after the death of his father is to treat his friends in a friendly manner (as the father would have done).

Show Allah ﷻ Your Good deeds in Ramadhaan

Ubaadah Ibn Saamit ؓ reports that, one day when Ramadhaan had come near, Rasulullah ﷺ said: "Ramadhaan, the month of blessings has come upon you, wherein Allah ﷻ turns towards you and sends to you His special blessings, forgives your faults, accepts your *duas*, appreciates your competing for the greatest good and boasts to the *Malaaikah* about you. So show to Allah ﷻ your good deeds; for truly, the most pitiful and unfortunate one is he who is deprived of Allah's ﷻ mercy in this month."

Note: In this *Hadeeth*, we read, about the spirit of competition among the believers, each one trying to do more good deeds than the other. In our home, I am greatly very happy at seeing how the women compete with each other, each one trying to recite more Qur'aan than the others, so that together with housework, each one reads half to two thirds of the Qur'aan daily. I mention this only out of a sense of gratitude to Allah ﷻ, indicating His favour and not to boast of it. May Allah ﷺ accept their and our actions, and increase our ability for good actions.

Freedom from Jahannam and Acceptance of Dua

Abu Saeed al-Khudree ؓ relates that Rasulullah ﷺ said: "During each day and night of Ramadhaan, Allah ﷻ sets free many people from *Jahannam,* and during each day and night, at least one *dua* for every Muslim is certainly accepted."

Note: Besides this *Hadeeth,* there are many others saying that the *dua* of a fasting person is accepted (*mustajaab*). In one *Hadeeth,* we read that the *dua* is accepted at the time of breaking the fast, but we are generally so busy eating, that we lose this chance.

The well known *dua* for breaking the fast is often forgotten:

اَللّٰهُمَّ لَكَ صُمْتُ وَبِكَ اٰمَنْتُ وَعَلٰى رِزْقِكَ اَفْطَرْتُ

"Allaahumma laka sumto wa bika aamantu wa alayka tawakkaltu wa alaa rizqika aftar tu"

(O Allah for You have I fasted, in You do I believe, and on You do I rely, and now I break this fast with food coming from You.)

Abdullah Ibn Amr ؓ used to make the following *dua* when breaking the fast.

اَللّٰهُمَّ اِنِّيۡ اَسۡئَلُكَ بِرَحۡمَتِكَ الَّتِيۡ وَسِعَتۡ كُلَّ شَيۡءٍ اَنۡ تَغۡفِرَ لِيۡ

"Allaa-humma innee as'aluka bi-rahmatikallatee wasita kulla shayin an taghfira lee"

(O Allah, I beg You, through Your infinite mercy, which surrounds all things, to forgive me.)

In some books we read that Rasulullah ﷺ used to say:

يَا وَا سِعَ الۡفَضۡلِ اِغۡفِرۡ لِيۡ

"Yaa waasi al-fadli-igh-firlee"

(O You who give Great Bounties, forgive me.)

There are many other *duas* for breaking the fast, but no special *dua* is fixed. This time (at breaking the fast) is a time when *duas* are accepted; ask and put all your needs before Allah ﷻ (and, if you remember, then make *dua* for me too).

Three Persons, whose Dua is surely accepted

Abu Hurairah رضي الله عنه reports that Rasulullah ﷺ said: "There are three persons whose *dua* is not rejected, The fasting person until he breaks the fast, the just ruler and the oppressed person, whose *dua* Allah ﷻ lifts above the clouds and opens to it the doors of *Jannah* and Allah ﷻ says, "I swear by my honour, verily, I shall assist you, even though it may be after sometime."

Note: It is reported from *Aa'isha* رضي الله عنها that, when Ramadhaan came, the colour of Rasulullah's ﷺ face used to change. He then used to increase his *Salaah*, become even more humble in his *dua* and show even more fear of Allah ﷻ.

According to another report, he hardly ever lay down in bed until Ramadhaan came to an end, Further, it is said that the *Malaaikah* carrying Allah's ﷻ throne are commanded in Ramadhaan to leave everything else and say '*Aameen*' to the *dua* of those who fast. There are many *Ahaadeeth* stating that the fasting person's *dua*s are answered. When Allah ﷻ has so promised and His truthful Nabi ﷺ has informed us, there should be no doubt whatsoever about the truth of these promises.

Yet it is strange that, in spite of this, we still find such people who do not get what they make *dua* for. They ask and do not receive, but this does not mean that their *dua* has been rejected. We should understand what is meant by a *dua* being answered.

Rasulullah ﷺ has told us that when a Muslim makes *dua* for anything from Allah ﷻ, as long as he does not make *dua* for breaking off relationship from his near relatives or for anything sinful, he definitely receives one out of the following three things: he gets the exact thing which he asked for. If that is not received, then Allah ﷻ either removes from him some great problem in exchange for what he wanted, or the reward for that thing for which he made *dua* for is stored for him in the *Aakhirah* (Hereafter).

Another *Hadeeth* says that on the day of *Qiyamah*, Allah ﷻ will call his slave and say to him: "O My slave, I used to command you to ask of Me and promised to answer. Did you beg of Me?" The slave will answer: "Yes I did." Then Allah ﷻ shall reply: "You did not make any *dua* which has not been accepted. You made *dua* that a certain problem should be removed, which I did for you in the worldly life.

You made *dua* that a certain sadness should be removed from you, but the result of that *dua* was not known to you. I have fixed for you such and such reward in the *Aakhirah* (Hereafter)."

Rasulullah ﷺ says that the man shall again be reminded of each and every *dua* and he shall be shown how it had been answered in the world or else what reward had been stored for him in the *Aakhirah* (Hereafter). On seeing that reward, he shall wish that not a single *dua* of his had been answered on earth, so that he could receive the full rewards only in the *Aakhirah* (Hereafter).

Yes, *dua* is indeed very important and to leave it out at any time is a great loss. Hope should not be lost, even when it seems that our *dua* is not accepted. Even from the long *Hadeeth* at the end of this book, it is clear that Allah ﷻ in accepting *dua*s considers, first of all, our own good. Should Allah ﷻ find that giving us what we ask from Him is for our own good, He gives it, otherwise not. Actually, it is Allah's ﷻ favour on us that we do not always get what we ask for because, very often, due to our lack of understanding, we beg for things that are not good for us at a particular time.

Here I must say that men as well as women have a bad habit of cursing their children in their anger. Beware of this. There are certain times when Allah ﷻ immediately accepts whatever *dua* is made. So sometimes, due to our own stupidity, the child is cursed and when the effect of that same curse comes upon the child and lands him into a big problem, the parents go about crying and complaining. Rasulullah ﷺ commanded us not to curse ourselves, our children, things that we own, or our servants.

It is just possible that the curse is said at a time when all *duas* are answered, especially in Ramadhaan, which is full of such special moments of acceptance. Hence, in this month great care should be taken.

Umar رضي الله عنه says that Rasulullah ﷺ said, "Whosoever remembers Allah ﷻ in Ramadhaan, is definitely forgiven and one who asks for a favour from Allah ﷻ, is not refused." Ibnu Masood ؓ says that, on every night of Ramadhaan, an Angel from the heavens calls out: "O You seeker of good, come near, O You seeker of evil, turn away (from evil) and open your eyes." Thereafter, that Angel calls out: "Is there any seeker of forgiveness, that he may be forgiven? Is there someone who would repent so that Allah ﷻ accepts his repentance? Is there anyone requesting a *dua*, that his *dua* may be heard? Is there anyone wanting anything, so that his wish may be answered?"

Lastly, it should be remembered that there are certain conditions under which *duas* are accepted. Without these, *duas* may often be rejected. Among these is the use of *halaal* and pure food. When food not permitted by Allah ﷻ is eaten, *duas* are not accepted.

Rasulullah ﷺ said: "Many a time a greatly troubled person lifts up his hands to the heavens, making *dua* and crying: 'O Allah!' but the food he eats is forbidden by Allah ﷻ , what he drinks is forbidden, his clothes have been earned by haraam means, then in such cases how can his *dua* be ever accepted?"

A story is related about a group of people in Kufa, whose *dua* used to be always accepted. Whenever a cruel ruler was put over them, they used to make *dua* for a curse upon him, which quickly came to destroy him. When Hajjaaj became the ruler there, he invited these people to a feast. After they had all eaten, he said: "I am no longer afraid of the curse upon me from these people, because *haraam* (forbidden) food has now entered their stomachs."

Let us think over how many things, forbidden by Allah ﷻ, are being eaten in these times, and people are even trying to make the taking of interest permissible. We find people going so far as to think that bribery and what is obtained through it is permissible, while our businessmen very often think it okay to bluff people when doing business with them.

Importance of Sehri (the meal before Dawn)

The mercy of Allah ﷻ and His Malaaikah are upon those who eat Sehri

Ibn Umar ؓ says that, Rasulullah ﷺ said: "Verily Allah ﷻ and His *Malaaikah* send blessings upon those who eat *Sehri*".

Note: How great is Allah's ﷻ favour upon us that even eating before dawn for fasting is so greatly rewarded. There are many *Ahaadeeth* in which the rewards of *sehri* are explained. Allama Ainee, a famous Aalim, has quoted the rewards of *sehri* from seventeen different *Sahaabah* ؓ.

Many people lose this great reward because of their own laziness. Some people, after finishing the *Taraweeh Salaat*, eat some food in place of *sehri* and go to bed. What great blessing do they lose! *Sehri* actually means food eaten shortly before dawn. Some ulema say that the time for *sehri* starts after midnight *(Mirqaat)*. The author of Al-Kashshaaf (Az-Zamakhsharee) divided the night into six parts, saying that the last one of these is the time of *sehri*. Therefore, when the night (from sunset till dawn) lasts twelve hours, the last two hours would be the correct time for *sehri.*

Then it must also be remembered that to eat at the last permissible time is better and greater in reward than eating earlier, on condition that *sehri* is completed before the time of dawn.

Rewards of Sehri

Nabi ﷺ said, "The difference between our fasting and that of the *Ahle Kitaab* (Jews and Christians) is that we eat *sehri* and they do not." Nabi ﷺ has said, "Eat *sehri*, because in it lies great blessings."

In another *Hadeeth* it is said, "In three things are great blessings, in *Jamaat* (in a group), in eating *thareed* (a special dish) and in *sehri.* In this *Hadeeth*, the use of the word *Jamaat* is general (for all actions), it includes *Salaah* with *Jamaat* and all those good actions done in a group, as Allah's ﷻ help comes to them.

Thareed is a type of tasty food, in which baked bread is cooked with meat. The third thing this *Hadeeth* speaks of is *sehri.* When Rasulullah ﷺ used to invite any of the *Sahaabah* رضي الله عنهم to eat *sehri* with him, he used to say: "Come and eat the blessed food with me."

One *Hadeeth* says: "Eat *sehri* and strengthen yourself for the fast, Sleep in the afternoon (siesta) to make it easy to wake up in the later portion of the night (for the worship of Allah ﷻ)." Abdullah Ibn Haarith reports that one of the *Sahaabah* رضي الله عنهم said, "I once visited Rasulullah ﷺ at a time when he was busy in eating *sehri.*" Rasulullah ﷺ then said: "This is a thing full of *barakah*, which Allah ﷻ has granted you. Do not give it up."

Rasulullah ﷺ in encouraging us repeatedly for *sehri* has said: "If there is nothing else, at least eat a date or drink some water." Thus, when there are definitely great advantages and reward in *sehri*, Muslims should try hard to partake in *sehri* as much as possible. However, in all things moderation (not too less or not too much) is important, and eating more than the required amount is harmful.

Neither should so little be eaten that one feels weak while fasting nor should so much be eaten that it causes discomfort. We have been advised not to overeat.

Ibn Hajar has listed different reasons regarding the *barakah* (blessings) of *sehri*:

a) The *Sunnah* is followed.
b) Through *sehri*, we seperate ourselves from the ways of *Ahle Kitaab* (Jews and Christians), which we are at all times supposed to do.
c) It provides strength for worship of Allah ﷻ.
d) It causes greater sincerity in the worship of Allah ﷻ.
e) It aids in preventing bad temper, which normally comes about as a result of hunger.
f) *Sehri* is the time when *duas* are accepted.
g) At the time of *sehri*, one gets the opportunity to remember Allah ﷻ, make *zikr* and *dua*.

In my opinion, the amount to be eaten is different according to different persons and their activities. For example, for those students who are busy studying the knowledge of *Deen*, too little food at *sehri* as well as at breaking the fast will be harmful for them. For them it is better not to eat too little, because they are studying religious knowledge, which is very important (for the protection and spread of Islam).

Similar is the case of those who are busy with *zikr* and other religious activities. Other people who have no such hard work to do should eat little at *sehri*.

Once, the Nabi ﷺ announced to those going for *jihad*; "There is no reward in fasting while travelling." That was in the month of Ramadhaan, when some *Sahaabah* ؓ were fasting. Of course, where one is doing some work of *Deen* where eating less does not lead to weakness, then it is best to eat less.

It is better that one should eat less in the nights of Ramadhaan than on other nights. After all, there is little benefit in fasting after having filled oneself at *sehri* and at breaking the fast. The pious people have said, “Whoever remains hungry in Ramadhaan shall remain safe from the evil of *Shaytaan* throughout the year until the next Ramadhaan.”

Many people Fast and Worship at Night but earn nothing besides Hunger and lost sleep

Abu Hurairah ﷺ relates that Rasulullah ﷺ said, “Many people who fast, get nothing for their fasting except hunger and many perform *Salaah* by night but get nothing by it except the discomfort of staying awake.”

Note: The Ulama have three different interpretations about this Hadeeth.

Firstly, this *Hadeeth* may mean that those who fast during the day and then for breaking the fast eat food that is *haraam*. All the reward for fasting is lost because of the greater sin of eating *haraam* food and nothing is gained except remaining hungry.

Secondly, it may mean those who fast but during fasting busy themselves in backbiting and falsely accusing others.

Thirdly, the person referred to may be one, who did not stay away from evil and sin while fasting.

In this *Hadeeth*, all such possibilities are included. Similar, is the case of the person performing *Salaah* the entire night but because of backbiting or any other sinful act (e.g. missing *Fajr Salaah* or keeping awake for show), loses the reward for his night of worship.

Fasting is a Protective Shield

Abu Ubaydah ﷺ reports, I have heard Rasulullah ﷺ saying, "Fasting is a protective shield for man, as long as he does not tear up that protection."

Note: "Protective Shield" means: Just as a man protects himself with a shield, similarly fasting protects him from his well known enemy *Shaitaan*. In other *Ahaadeeth*, we are told that fasting saves one from Allah's ﷻ punishment and the fire of *Jahannam* in the *Aakhirah* (Hereafter).

Once, somebody asked Rasulullah ﷺ, "What causes the fast to be torn?" He ﷺ replied, "Speaking lies and backbiting." This *Hadeeth*, when read alone with many others, actually tells us not to do those things which causes the fast to be wasted.

In our times, we are fond of wasting time with unnecessary conversations. Some *Ulama'* say that lies, backbiting, slander (wrongly accusing somebody) etc. actually break the fast just like eating and drinking. But the *Ulama'* believe that the fast is not totally broken, but loses its blessing (*barakah*). The *Ulama'* of Islam tell us of six things, about which care should be taken in fasting:

Firstly: one should keep the eyes away from any place where one should not look. Some go so far as to forbid looking at one's own wife with desire, let alone another woman. Similarly, looking at any evil action or where evil is committed should be avoided. (e.g. T.V, DVD's, etc)

Rasulullah ﷺ said: "to look in the wrong place is like an arrow from *Shaitaan*. Whosoever, out of fear of Allah ﷻ protects his gaze; Allah ﷻ shall give him such *noor* (light) of *Imaan*, the taste and sweetness of which he will feel in the heart."

The pious people say that this means that we should not look at all at those places and things that take the mind away from the remembrance of Allah ﷻ.

Secondly: One should guard the tongue from lies, unnecessary talks, backbiting, arguments, etc. In the Saheeh Bukhari we read that fasting is a shield for the fasting person, for this reason, those who fast should stay away from all useless talk, joking, arguments, etc. Should anyone start an argument, then say to him, "I am fasting."

In other words, one should not start an argument and if someone else starts it, then too, one should avoid taking it up. When the person who starts an argument is not an understanding person, then at least one should remind oneself that: "I am fasting."

During the time of our Nabi ﷺ, two women were fasting and they felt so hungry that they could not manage the fast and both were close to death. When the *Sahaabah* رضي الله عنهم told our Nabi ﷺ about this, he sent a bowl to the women asking both of them to vomit into it. When they both vomited into the bowl, pieces of meat and fresh blood were found in it. The *Sahaabah* رضي الله عنهم were greatly surprised, upon which our Nabi ﷺ said: "They fasted with pure food from Allah ﷻ, but ate food not permitted by Allah ﷻ by backbiting other people."

From the above we see that, by backbiting during fasting, the fast becomes more difficult. For this reason both women were close to death. Similar is the case with other sinful acts. However, fasting is not difficult for the pious Allah-fearing persons, whereas the sinful people find it very difficult. One should therefore, stay away from sins and especially major sins like backbiting and slander, which are often done to pass time. Allah ﷻ says in the Qur'aan that backbiting is the (actual) eating of the flesh of one's dead brother.

One of the *Sahaabah* رضي الله عنه asked Rasulullah ﷺ, "What is backbiting?" Rasulullah ﷺ replied: "To say something about your brother, behind his back, which he would not like." The *Sahaabah* رضي الله عنه then said: "And is it still backbiting if what is said about him is really true?" Our Nabi ﷺ said: "In that case (if that which was said is really true) it is exactly backbiting; but if what is said is false, then you have in fact slandered (falsely accused) him."

Once when Nabi ﷺ passed by two graves, He said: "Punishment is being given to both the people of these graves. One is being punished because of backbiting and the other because of not having taken precautions (to stay clean) when passing urine."

Thirdly: The person who fasts must be careful about what he hears. Whatever is wrong to say, is also wrong to listen too. Rasulullah ﷺ has said, "In backbiting, both the backbiter and the one who listens to it are equal in sin."

Fourthly: The rest of the body should be kept away from sin and wrong things. The hands must not touch it and the feet must not walk towards it. Special care should be taken especially at the time of breaking the fast that no doubtful food enters the stomach. When a person fasts and at the time of breaking the fast, breaks his fast with *haraam* food, he is like a sick person who takes medicine as a cure but also adds a little poison, which kills him.

Fifthly: After having fasted, it is not good while breaking the fast at *iftaar* to completely fill the stomach even with *halaal* food because the purpose of fasting is then lost. Fasting decreases your bodily needs and increases a persons faith and piety.

For eleven months, we eat and drink freely. In Ramadhaan this should be cut down to a minimum. We have a bad habit of filling our stomachs when breaking the fast to cover up for what was lost and again at *sehri* in preparation for the fast, thereby actually increasing our daily food.

Ramadhaan for such people increases their appetite. Many such items of food are eaten that we normally do not eat at other times. This type of habit is completely against the spirit of Ramadhaan and the true spirit of fasting.

Imam Ghazali رَحْمَةُ اللهِ عَلَيْه asks the same question: "When the object of fasting is to decrease our bodily needs and to go against *Shaitaan*, how can this possibly be done by overeating when breaking the fast?"

Actually in that case we have only changed the times of eating and not really fasted. In fact, by having many types of delicious foods, we eat even more than in normal times. The result is that instead of lessening the bodily desires, these are increased. The real benefit of fasting comes with real hunger. Our Nabi ﷺ said, "*Shaitaan* lives in the body of man like blood, so close up his path by remaining hungry," i.e. when the body is hungry, the spirit receives strength.

Apart from hunger, fasting gives us a chance to see the condition of the poor people and thereby feeling sorry for them. This too can be felt by remaining hungry, but by filling the stomach with delicious foods at *sehri*, we will be losing the purpose of fasting because we will not feel hungry throughout the fast.

In one kitaab it is written: "Do not overeat at *sehri*, as this is a way to lose the object of fasting." An Alim writes, "The reward for fasting becomes more when hunger is really felt. Similarly, we feel sorry for the poor and hungry ones."

Our Nabi ﷺ himself said: "Allah ﷻ does not hate the filling of anything to the top more than He hates the filling of the stomach." Rasulullah ﷺ said, "A few bites should be enough to keep the back straight. The best way for man is that one third should be filled with food, one third with drink, while the other third remains empty." Rasulullah ﷺ himself used to fast for days together without having eaten inbetween.

The sixth point is that: After fasting, we should always worry about whether our fast had been accepted by Allah ﷻ or not. This should be done with all forms of *ibaadaat* (worship) of Allah ﷻ. We never know whether something important may have been left out by mistake. We should always fear that Allah ﷻ may not accept our actions. Rasulullah ﷺ said: "Many reciters of the Qur'aan are being cursed by the Qur'aan."

Rasulullah ﷺ also said: "On the day of *Qiyaamah*, one of those whom Allah ﷻ shall question first shall be a martyr (a person who died in the path of Allah ﷻ). Allah ﷻ shall call him and remind him of all His favours to him which he shall admit. He shall then be asked: 'What have you done to show thanks for these favours?' The martyr shall reply: 'I fought for Your sake till I was martyred.' Allah ﷻ shall reply; 'It is not so, you fought so that you can be called a brave man and so it has been said.' Thereafter, it shall be commanded that he be dragged face on the ground and thrown into *Jahannam*.' Thereafter, a religious scholar shall be called. He too, shall be reminded of Allah's ﷻ favours and asked the same question. He shall reply: 'O Allah! I worked hard to get Deeni knowledge, taught others and for Your sake and recited the Qur'aan.' Allah ﷻ shall say; 'This is not true. You did all that only so that it may be said that you are learned and so it has been said.' Then it shall be commanded that he too be dragged face on the ground and thrown into *Jahannam*. Thereafter, a rich man shall be called. After being reminded of Allah's ﷻ favours and admitting them, in reply to Allah's ﷻ question as to what he did to show his thanks, he shall reply, 'There was no good cause where I did not spend in charity for Your sake.' Allah's ﷻ reply shall be, 'Not true, you did all that, so that it may be said that you are very generous and so it has been said.' Then it shall be commanded that he too be dragged face on the ground and thrown into *Jahannam*."

Many such incidents are related in *Ahaadeeth*. So, a fasting person should not only be sincere but also hope that Allah ﷻ will accept his fast.

These six points are compulsory for all truly righteous persons. As for the very pious ones, a seventh point is added. That is during fasting, the heart should not be turned towards anyone except Allah

ﷻ, so much so that during the fast there should be no worry as to whether there shall be something to eat for breaking the fast.

Some *Mashaaikh* even consider it a fault to think about food for breaking the fast or that one should try to get something because this shows lack of faith in Allah's ﷻ promise of being responsible for taking care of all our needs.

The Qur'aan commands, ***"Fasting has been made fardh for you."*** From this *Aayah* it is seen that fasting is made compulsory for every part of the body. Thus, fasting of the tongue means to avoid lies, etc., fasting of the ears means not listening to evil, fasting of the eyes means not to look at any form of evil and sin. Similarly; fasting of the self means to be free from all bodily desires, fasting of the heart means removing the love of worldly things from it and fasting of the mind means avoiding thoughts about anything other than Allah ﷻ.

A single fast of Ramadhaan is more valuable than a lifetime of fasts kept out of Ramadhaan

Abu Hurairah رضي الله عنه reports that Rasulullah ﷺ said: "Whosoever eats during one day of Ramadhaan without a valid excuse (acceptable in *Shari'ah*) shall never be able to get back that day even by fasting for the rest of his life."

Note: Some *Ulama'* say that when anybody, without any valid excuse, did not fast on any day of Ramadhaan, he can never make up that day of Ramadhaan which was lost even if he fasts for the rest of his life. Ali رضي الله عنه held this view. However, most of the *Ulama'* say that if a person did not fast for one day of Ramadhaan then to make up, he will have to fast for only one day. On the other hand, if a person had started a fast in Ramadhaan and had then broken it knowingly during the day without any valid excuse, then according to the *Shari'ah* he shall have to fast for sixty days one after the other with *sehri* and *iftaar*. However, the full reward and blessings of Ramadhaan will never be obtained. This is the meaning of the above *Hadeeth* i.e. where a day of Ramadhaan had been lost without excuse, no matter how many days he fasts later, he will never be able to make up the true blessings of a single day of fasting in Ramadhaan.

All this is for those who try to make up their lost days of fasting. How unfortunate and misguided are those who completely ignore the fast and do not fast at all in Ramadhaan nor fast thereafter as *kaffaarah* (covering up).

Fasting is one of the pillars of Islam and Rasulullah ﷺ has told us of five such pillars. First is the oneness of Allah ﷻ and the *Nubuwwah* of Muhammad ﷺ and thereafter the four remaining pillars *Salaah*, fasting, *Zakaah* and Hajj.

Ibn Abbas رضي الله عنه relates a *Hadeeth* saying: "Islam is based on three things (1) *Imaan* (2) *Salaah* (3) Fasting. Whoever ignores any one of these is a disbeliever and deserves severe punishment." The *Ulama'* have said that a person only becomes a disbeliever when he fails to do that action and in addition he also denies it being a part of Deen.

There are those ignorant persons who do not fast but much worse is the case of those who not only refuse to fast but they make fun of the month of fasting e.g. by saying in a mocking manner, "He should fast who has no food in his house," or "What does Allah ﷻ gain by making us suffer from hunger?"

Such words should never be said, it should be remembered that to make fun of the smallest of part our *Deen* can lead to *kufr* (disbelief). Should any person not perform a single *Salaah* in his life, not fast one single day or fail to perform any *fardh* actions in Islam, he does not become a *kaafir* provided he does not deny these actions to be necessary. He shall be punished for whatever fardh action that has left out.

Anyone failing to fast in Ramadhaan without a valid excuse is disobedient to Allah ﷻ. Some scholars of Islamic law have gone so far as to state that anyone eating publicly (in front of others) in Ramadhaan, without a valid excuse, should be put to death.

At least we should consider such actions bad. I consider these ten *Ahaadeeth* sufficient in this first chapter for those who wish to follow them sincerely. As for those who have no intention to change their actions accordingly, no amount of writing will be useful, May Allah ﷻ grant me and all Muslims the strength to do good deeds, because we all have our faults. (*Aameen*)

Laylatul Qadr

Amongst the nights of Ramadhaan, there is one called '*Laylatul Qadr*,' a night of great blessings. The *Qur'aan-e-Kareem* describes it as being greater in blessedness and rewards than a thousand months which means that it is greater than eighty three years and four months.

Fortunate is that person who gets the full blessings of this night by spending it in *ibaadah* of Allah ﷻ, because he has then earned reward for *ibaadah* of eighty-three years and four months and even more. Indeed the granting of this night to the Muslims is a great favour.

The Origin

In a *Hadeeth* reported by Anas ؓ, Rasulullah ﷺ is reported to have said, "*Laylatul Qadr* was given to my *ummah* and not to any other *ummah* before this." Many reasons for the granting of *Laylatul Qadr* have been mentioned. One reason, according to some *Ahaadeeth* is given thus: Rasulullah ﷺ used to look at the longer lives of the earlier people and was saddened over the shorter lives of his own *ummah*. If His *ummah* had wished to compete with the people before them in the doing of good deeds, because of their shorter lives, it would be impossible for them to either copy or beat them. To cover up for this difference in their shorter lives, Allah ﷻ in His countless mercy gave them this night of great blessings. This means that if any fortunate person of this *ummah* spends during his life time ten such nights in the worship of Allah ﷻ, he would have earned the reward for *ibaadah* of eight hundred and thirty years and even more.

Rasulullah ﷺ once related to the *Sahaabah* ﷺ the story of a very pious man from the Bani Israel, who used to spend one thousand months in *jihad*. On hearing this, the *Sahaabah* ﷺ envied that person because they could not get the same reward whereupon Allah ﷻ granted them *Laylatul Qadr* (the Night of Power).

Our Nabi ﷺ once mentioned the names of the four most pious people from amongst the Bani Israel who each spent eighty years in Allah ﷻ sincere *ibaadah*, worshipping Him, and not sinning at all. They were Nabi Ayyub عليه السلام, Zakariyya عليه السلام, Hizqeel عليه السلام and Yushaa عليه السلام. The *Sahaabah* ﷺ heard this with astonishment. Then Jibraeel عليه السلام appeared and recited *Surah Qadr*, where the blessings of this night were revealed.

This is a great favour and gift of Allah ﷻ. To make lots of *ibaadah* on this night is also a blessing from Allah ﷻ. How wonderful are those Pious Saints who did not miss the *ibaadah* of even one *Laylatul Qadr* since from a young age. Now, as to which night it is, approximately fifty different views of the *Ulama'* are mentioned. The numerous benefits of this night are mentioned in many books of *Hadeeth*. The Qur'aan *Majeed* itself mentions the night in *Surah Qadr*, of which we shall begin with a short commentary.

إِنَّا أَنزَلْنَٰهُ فِي لَيْلَةِ ٱلْقَدْرِ ۝١

(In the name of Allah the beneficent, the Merciful, We have indeed revealed this (message) in the night of Power. (Suratul Qadr: 1)

On this special night, the Qur'aan was sent down from the *lowhul mahfuz* (The preserved Tablet in a special place above the heavens) to the heavens above the earth. A great book like the *Qur'aan-e-kareem* being revealed on this night is sufficient to explain its excellence, not to mention all its other blessings and virtues. In the very next verse a question is asked.

وَمَآ اَدْرٰىكَ مَا لَيْلَةُ الْقَدْرِ ۝٢

And what will explain to you what the Night of Power is?

(Suratul Qadr: 2)

In other words, the question asked here is: Have you any knowledge as to the greatness and the great importance of this night? Have you any knowledge as to the great favours and gifts that are placed in it? The next verse tells us some of that greatness:

لَيْلَةُ الْقَدْرِ ۙ خَيْرٌ مِّنْ اَلْفِ شَهْرٍ ۝٣

The Night of Power is better than a thousand months.

(Suratul Qadr: 3)

The true meaning here is that the reward for spending this night in *ibaadah* is better than having spent one thousand months in *ibaadah.* It is in fact much more, but as to how much more rewarding it is, we are not told here.

تَنَزَّلُ الْمَلٰٓئِكَةُ وَالرُّوْحُ فِيْهَا بِاِذْنِ رَبِّهِمْ ۚ مِنْ كُلِّ اَمْرٍ ۝٤

Therein come down the Malaaikah and the Spirit by Allah's ﷻ permission on every task (Suratul Qadr: 4)

A good explanation is given on this verse by Imaam Raazi رَحْمَةُ اللهِ عَلَيْهِ. He explains that when man first appeared on earth, created by Allah ﷻ as His deputy on earth, the *Malaaikah* looked at man with doubt. When Allah ﷻ informed them of His intention of placing man on earth, they even went further to ask, "Will you place someone on this earth who shall commit evil and shed blood?"

On this Night of Power we see that same man worshipping Allah ﷻ and loving Him. Those very same *Malaaikah* who had before looked down on him with scorn, come down towards him, clearly sorry for the thoughts they had against him.

In this verse mention is made.... "and the spirit". Reference is clearly to Jibraeel عَلَيْهِ السَّلَامُ. Commentators of the Qur'aan have given many meanings of this word. The view we wish to mention here is that "Spirit" means Allah's ﷻ special mercy which comes when the *Malaaikah* come down.

Imaam Bayhaqi رَحْمَةُ اللهِ عَلَيْهِ reports a *Hadeeth* by Anas رَضِيَ اللهُ عَنْهُ wherein Rasulullah ﷺ is reported to have said, "On *Laylatul Qadr*, Jibraeel عَلَيْهِ السَّلَامُ comes down with a group of *Malaaikah* and makes *dua* of mercy for every one whom they find busy in *ibaadah.*"

This same verse which is being discussed says, "By Allah's permission on every task....

The Author of Mazhaairrul Haq writes that on this night ages ago the *Malaaikah* were created. On this night long ago the creation of Adam عَلَيْهِ السَّلَامُ began as the things from which he was created had been gathered on this night. Trees were planted in *Jannah* and a large number of *Ahaadeeth* state clearly that on this night *dua's* are accepted.

سَلٰمٌ ۛ هِيَ حَتّٰى مَطْلَعِ الْفَجْرِ ۝٥

Peace be until the break of dawn (Suratul Qadr: 5)

Yes, this is the very picture of peace. Throughout the night the *Malaaikah* recite *salaam* on the true believers who love their Lord. As one group come down another goes up as is explained in the *Ahaadeeth.* Another meaning is that it is a night of complete safety from evil and mischief. These blessings remain throughout the night until the break of dawn and are not limited to any particular hour.

Having noted a few virtues of this night as explained in the words of Allah ﷻ, we now turn to the *Hadeeth* where we read more about the virtues of this night.

All Sins are Forgiven on Worshipping during this Night

Abu Hurairah ؓ reports that Rasulullah ﷺ said, "Whoever stands in prayer and *ibaadah* on the 'Night of Power' with sincere faith and with sincere hope of gaining reward, his previous sins are forgiven." (Targheeb from Bukhari and Muslim)

Commentary

In the above *Hadeeth* "standing" refers to *Salaah* as well as any other form of *ibaadah,* for example *zikr, tilaawat* etc. The phrase '...with sincere hope of gaining reward,' means that we should be sincerely occupied with *ibaadah* only for the pleasure of Allah ﷻ and to receive reward from Him. This should not be done for others to see, or to deceive them. According to Khataabi, it means that we should have complete faith in the promise that any action shall be rewarded and thus one must stand before Allah ﷻ with seriousness and eagerness. Neither should we think of this *ibaadah* as a great difficulty nor should there be any doubt about the reward which will be granted to us.

The *Hadeeth* speaks about previous sins being forgiven. The *Ulama'* have said that this forgiveness mentioned in the above *Hadeeth* and other *Ahaadeeth*, refers only to minor (small) sins. According to the Qur'aan, major (big) sins can only be forgiven after sincere *taubah* (repentance) with the promise never to do such sins again. This is the reason why the *Ulama'* have agreed that major sins are not forgiven except by sincere repentance. Hence, whenever forgiveness of sins is mentioned in the *Ahaadeeth*, the *Ulama'* specify it to be minor sins.

My late father (May Allah ﷻ bless him and grant him *noor* in his resting place) used to say that the word 'minor' has been left out, because a true Muslim is one on whom there should be no major sins. Whenever a major sin has been committed, he will never rest or find peace until he has sincerely repented and begged Allah ﷻ for forgiveness and promised not to do the same in future.

When a night like *Laylatul Qadr* comes along, one who has committed major sins should first of all ask for forgiveness with a heart full of sincerity, so that Allah ﷻ in His infinite mercy may forgive all forms of sins and when you do, remember me too in your *dua*'s (The publishers and myself request the same).

To lose Laylatul Qadr is to lose all good

Anas ؓ reports that once when Ramadhaan had begun, Rasulullah ﷺ said: "A month has verily come upon you, which has a night better than a thousand months. Whoever misses such a night has lost all that is good and none loses, except he who is really unfortunate."

Note: Who can have any doubt as to the misfortune of the person who loses the great good of *Laylatul Qadr*? There are those who, during their jobs, have to stay awake by night throughout the year. How easy should it be for the sake of gaining the reward of over eighty years of worship of Allah ﷻ to stay awake for one month in Allah's ﷻ service?

Because of no interest, there is no desire in the heart to do *Ibaadah.* If that were present, then even a thousand nights worshipping Allah ﷻ would become very easy. It is this urge and desire that we must create. Our Nabi ﷺ had been promised many times that he had nothing to fear in the *Aakhirah* (Hereafter) and had been given good news as to his high position. Yet night after night he was seen standing for long periods and worshipping Allah ﷻ so much that his feet would become swollen. Among the believers of Islam, there are many pious saints who copied his example. They were human beings like us and no one can say that it is impossible for us to have that same desire for worship. It is really a matter of taking this to heart. Let us look at the example of the following famous pious people of Islam. One such person was Umar رضي الله عنه, who having performed his *Esha Salaah* would return home and then remain in *Salaah* throughout the night until the *Azaan* was heard for *Fajr.* Then there is the example of Usman رضي الله عنه who, after fasting the whole day used to spend the whole night in *Salaah* besides getting a little sleep during the first third of the night. It is well known about him that he used to recite the whole Qur'aan in one *rakaat.*

Ibrahim Ibn Adham رَحْمَةُ اللهِ عَلَيْه went so far as not to sleep at all in Ramadhaan, night or Day. Imam Shaafi رَحْمَةُ اللهِ عَلَيْه used to recite the Qur'aan about sixty times during the days and nights of Ramadhaan. Besides these, there were countless other pious people who used to act carefully on the order of the Qur'aanic *Ayah*:

I have created the Jinn and Humans only that they may worship Me". (Surah Al-Zaariyaat: 56)

These are some examples of the people of the past. Even in times of evil and corruption, there are people who truly try to follow the example of Rasulullah ﷺ and do not let their jobs or their comforts stop them from worshipping Allah تعالى. Rasulullah ﷺ said that Allah تعالى says: "O son of Adam, spend your time in My worship and I shall bless you with freedom from want and I shall remove your poverty. Otherwise, I shall load you with lots of work and duties, while your poverty and needs shall not decrease." How often we see the truth of this. Some people serve only Allah تعالى while having no job and yet we see that they do not need anything.

The Malaaikah Coming Down

Anas رضي الله عنه reports that Rasulullah ﷺ said: "On *Laylatul Qadr*, Jibraeel عليه السلام comes down upon the earth with a group of *Malaaikah*, making *dua* for blessings for every servant of Allah تعالى whom they see in worship, standing or sitting and engaged in Allah's تعالى praise. Then, on the day of *Eid*, Allah تعالى boasts about them to the *Malaaikah* (who were not too happy at the time of Adam's عليه السلام creation): 'O My *Malaaikah*, what is the reward of that worker who had done his job very well?' They reply: 'O Allah! his reward should be given to him in full.' To this Allah تعالى replies, 'O My *Malaaikah*, My servants, the males as well as the females, have today done their duty, thereafter they went to the place of *Eid Salaah* (*Eid Gha*) raising their voices in *dua* to Me. I swear by My Honour, by My Greatness, by My Grace and by My High Position, that I shall surely answer the *dua*'s of these people.' Thereafter, Allah تعالى addresses the people: 'Go, I have forgiven your sins and have replaced your evil actions with good ones.' These people then return from the place of *Eid Salaah* in such a condition that their sins are forgiven."

Note: In this *Hadeeth*, it is clearly stated that Jibraeel عليه السلام comes down with the *Malaaikah*. Another *Hadeeth* reported by Ibn Abbas رضي الله عنه and quoted by Abdul Qadir Jilani رحمة الله عليه in his book Ghunyah, further explains this *Hadeeth*.

It is reported that Jibraeel ﷺ, after coming down, commands the *Malaaikah* to go to the house of everyone busy with worship of Allah ﷻ and greet him by shaking his hands. Then the *Malaaikah* spread out, visiting every house, whether large or small, whether in the jungle or on a ship, wherever a believer lives, to shake his hands. However, certain houses are not entered; the house where a dog or pig is found, the house where there is someone who has committed adultery *(zina)* and is still unclean because he has not even taken a bath and the house where pictures (photos) of men and animals are displayed.

How sad it is that Muslim houses should lose the blessed visit of the *Malaaikah* only because there are pictures of men and animals being displayed for the sake of decoration. A single picture may have been hung by just one person of the house, as a result of which all the other people in the house are deprived of blessings.

When to look for Laylatul Qadr?

Aa'isha رضي الله عنها reports that Rasulullah ﷺ said, "Look for *Laylatul Qadr* during the odd numbered nights of the last ten days of the month of Ramadhaan."

Note: According to most of the *ulema,* the last ten nights start on the 21st night, whether the month of Ramadhaan has of 29 or 30 days. So, we should look for Laylatul Qadr on the 21st, 23rd, 25th, 27th and 29th night.

Ibn Hazm has a different opinion saying that the word *Asharah* used in the *Hadeeth* means ten. Thus, the above calculations will only be correct where the month of Ramadhaan has thirty days. However, when there are only twenty nine days in the month (as often happens), the last ten days will start with the 19th day and the night being the 20th night. According to this calculation, it would mean that the odd numbered nights will actually be the 20th, 22nd, 24th, 26th and 28th nights.

However, all the *Ulama'* agree that when Rasulullah ﷺ went into *i'tikaaf* in search of *Laylatul Qadr*, he started it on the 21st night of Ramadhaan. Therefore, these *Ulama'* consider the odd nights to be the appropriate nights for *Laylatul Qadr*.

We should therefore spend each and every night from the 20th onwards worshipping Allah ﷻ, so that we may be sure of getting the *barakah* of Ramadhaan. Spending ten or eleven nights in worship is definitely not so difficult, if we look at the great reward that is promised.

Exact Knowledge of the date of Laylatul Qadr taken away

Ubaadah Ibn Saamit ؓ said, "Once Nabi ﷺ came out to inform us of the (correct date of) *Laylatul Qadr*. Unfortunately, a quarrel between two Muslims took place and Nabi ﷺ said, 'I came out to inform you as to when *Laylatul Qadr* occurs, but because two people quarrelled with each other, the knowledge of the correct date was taken away. Perhaps that is better for you. So, look for it in the ninth, seventh and fifth nights.'"

Note: Three important points are referred to in this *Hadeeth*. Firstly it tells us of a quarrel, as a result of which the knowledge of the exact night of *Laylatul Qadr* was lost to us. Arguments and quarrels always cause the loss of blessings.

Once Rasulullah ﷺ asked the *Sahaabah* ؓ: "Shall I inform you of something that is better than *Salaah*, fasting and charity?" The *Sahaabah* ؓ replied: "Certainly." Rasulullah ﷺ then said, "Do keep peaceful and good relations amongst yourselves, because quarrelling destroys (shave off) faith *(Imaan).*" This means that just as a razor shaves off the hair, so does quarrelling affects our *Deen.*

Nowadays besides the worldly people, even those who seem to be pious are also involved in fighting. In the first chapter of this book, we read how Rasulullah ﷺ said that to insult a Muslim is a serious crime and equal to the worst kind of interest, but we are not at all worried. The orders of Allah ﷻ and His Rasul ﷺ are taken lightly.

The Qur'aan says:

"Do not argue among yourselves, otherwise you will lose courage and your strength will go away" (Surah al-Anfaal: 46).

Those who harm others are actually harming themselves. They have destroyed themselves in the eyes of Allah ﷻ and all those around them.

Rasulullah ﷺ said that the person, who refuses to speak to a Muslim brother for more than three days and dies in this condition, will go straight to *Jahannam.* It is stated in another *Hadeeth* that, on every Monday and Thursday, the actions of human beings are brought before Allah ﷻ. Then forgiveness is granted through His mercy (as a result of certain good deeds), except to those who worship idols and those who join partners to Allah ﷻ. However, when two friends have a fight and then stop being friends, it will be said, "Leave them until they again become friends."

Another *Hadeeth* states that, when our actions are shown to Allah ﷻ every Monday and Thursday, repentance is accepted from those who repent and forgiveness is granted to those who seek pardon. As for those who had arguments (with each other) they are left as they were.

A *Hadeeth* further teaches us that, on the night of *Shabe Baraat* (the 15th night of Shabaan), the mercy of Allah ﷻ is sent to all Allah's

ﷻ creation and forgiveness is freely granted, except for two persons: A nonbeliever and one who has evil thoughts about others.

In another *Hadeeth* it is stated: "There are three people whose *Salaah* does not lift even a span (size of a hand) above their heads." One of these people are those who quarrel among themselves.

This *Hadeeth* also tells us that we should be satisfied and accept Allah's ﷻ decision in all things. For example, even though it seems that not knowing when *Laylatul Qadr* actually falls is a great loss, yet it has to be accepted because it is from Allah ﷻ. Because of this, Rasulullah ﷺ said. "It is better for us that way." We should think about this, as Allah ﷻ is Merciful to us at all times. Even when someone is given a great punishment because of his own evil deeds, he only needs to beg Allah ﷻ, admit his own evil deeds, admit his own weakness and that same punishment becomes the cause for great good. Nothing is impossible for Allah ﷻ.

Our *Ulama'* have pointed out quite a few advantages in our not knowing the exact date for *Laylatul Qadr*. First, had we known the actual date of this blessed night, there would have been many who would not have worshipped Allah ﷻ at all during the other nights. Therefore, we have to stay awake and worship Allah ﷻ for quite a number of nights, hoping that each night is perhaps the night of *Laylatul Qadr*. This means spending more nights in Allah's ﷻ worship and getting extra rewards.

Secondly, there are many of us those who are just not able to stay away from evil. How extremely dangerous and unfortunate for them would it be, when, in spite of knowing that such and such a night is *Laylatul Qadr*, they might still spend it in sin and evil? Once the Nabi ﷺ on entering the *Musjid*, saw one of the *Sahaabah* رضي الله عنه sleeping, He said to Ali رضي الله عنه, "Wake him up so that he can make *wudhu*". Ali رضي الله عنه obeyed and asked the Nabi ﷺ: "O Rasul of Allah ﷻ, you are always the first to rush towards any good deed. Why then did you not wake him up yourself?" Nabi ﷺ replied: "I feared that this man may refuse and refusal to my command is *kufr* (Denial of *Deen*). If he had refused your command, it would not be Kufr."

Similarly, Allah ﷻ, in His mercy, does not wish that, in spite of knowing which night is the real one, a Muslim should still spend it in sin and evil.

Thirdly, if we did know and in spite of that, for one reason or another, within or outside our control, we allowed that night to go by without worship of Allah ﷻ then it is very likely that thereafter, for the rest of Ramadhaan, no other night would have been spent in worship, whereas now many people find it possible to spend one, two or three nights in worship of Allah ﷻ because we do not know which is *Laylatul Qadr*.

Fourthly, every night spent in worship of Allah ﷻ looking for *Laylatul Qadr* is a night for which a separate reward is promised.

Fifthly, we have read that Allah ﷻ speaks highly to His *Malaaikah* about those believers who try very hard in worshipping Allah ﷻ during Ramadhaan, now more occasions of receiving Allah's ﷻ appreciation come about. In spite of not knowing when the real night of *Laylatul Qadr* is and although they have only an unclear idea about its fixed time, they still try hard to worship Allah ﷻ, night after night. If this is how they try when *Laylatul Qadr* is not known, how much more will they try if they knew?

The third point in the *Hadeeth* is that *Laylatul Qadr* should be found among three nights: The ninth, seventh and fifth. By reading this together with the other *Ahaadeeth*, we come to know that this refers to the last ten nights of Ramadhaan. So to work out which nights these are, if we start from the 20th, counting upwards, then these three nights are the 25th, 27th and 29th. If, on the other hand, we start counting from the 29th backwards (where Ramadhaan has 29 days) these nights would be the 21st, 23rd and 25th, but if

Ramadhaan has 30 days, then these would be the 22nd, 24th and 26th nights.

From this we can see how much uncertainty there is about the correct date. In fact, among the learned *Ulama'*, there are approximately fifty different opinions. Because of this, some *Ulama'* have said *Laylatul Qadr* does not fall on one and the same night every year. If in this particular year, it falls on a particular night, then the following year it will fall on another night.

There are times when the Nabi ﷺ commanded the *Sahaabah* ؓ to search among a number of nights, whereas at other times he used to fix a certain night.

Abu Hurairah ؓ reports that once during a conversation with the *Sahaabah* ؓ, someone spoke of *Laylatul Qadr*. Rasulullah ﷺ asked: "What is the date today?" They replied: "The 22nd of Ramadhaan." Nabi ﷺ said: "Search for *Laylatul Qadr* in the night following this day."

Abu Zarr ؓ reports, "I asked Nabi ﷺ whether *Laylatul Qadr* was only granted during the lifetime of Rasulullah ﷺ or whether it would continue to come after him, Rasulullah ﷺ replied: 'It will continue until the day of *Qiyamah.*' I then inquired in which section of Ramadhaan it comes. Nabi ﷺ replied, 'Search for it in the first ten and in the last ten days.' Thereafter Nabi ﷺ became busy with other work. I waited and finding another chance inquired: In which section of those ten days does *Laylatul Qadr* comes? Upon this, Rasulullah ﷺ became angry with me, as He had never been before and said, 'If it had been Allah's ﷻ wish to make it known, would He not have informed us? Search for it among the last seven nights, and ask no more."

In another *Hadeeth* again, Rasulullah ﷺ is reported to have told one *Sahaabi* ؓ that *Laylatul Qadr* was on the 23rd night. Ibn Abbas ؓ related: "Once, while sleeping, someone said to me in my dream: 'Rise up, this is *Laylatul Qadr*,' I woke up and rushed to Rasulullah

ﷺ who was busy in Salaah. That was the 23rd night." According to other reports, the 24th was *Laylatul Qadr*. Abdullah Ibn Masood ؓ said: "Whoever spends all the nights of the year in the worship of Allah ﷻ, can find *Laylatul Qadr*. (In other words, the blessed night moves throughout the year and does not necessarily have to come in Ramadhaan only)."

When this was related to Ubay Ibn Kaab ؓ he said: "Yes, Ibn Masood ؓ meaning is that people may not stay awake just on this night and become contented." Thereafter he swore by Allah ﷻ that *Laylatul Qadr* comes on the 27th. This view is also held by numerous *Sahaabah* ؓ and *Taabieen* (companions of the *Sahaabah* ؓ).

Most of the *Ulama'* also consider it most likely that, *Laylatul Qadr* comes every year on the 27th night (of Ramadhaan).

Therefore, if by good fortune we are blessed with finding the night, then it would outweigh all comforts and enjoyable things in the world. Even if we fail to get the much searched for night, then at least the reward for the worship is received. At least, effort should be made that the *Salaah* of *Maghrib* and *Esha* throughout the year is performed with *Jamaat* because if it is *Laylatul Qadr*, then the reward for both is so much more.

Signs of Laylatul Qadr

Ubadah Ibn Saamit ؓ reports that he asked Rasulullah ﷺ about *Laylatul Qadr*, Rasulullah ﷺ replied, "It is in Ramadhaan, during the last ten nights, on the odd numbered nights, either the 21st, 23rd, 25th, 27th or the last night of Ramadhaan. Whosoever stands up in the worship of Allah ﷻ on this night, with sincere faith *(Imaan)* and with genuine hopes of gaining reward, his previous sins will be forgiven. Among the signs of this night is that it is a peaceful, quiet, shining night, neither hot, nor cold but moderate as if a moon is shining clear and no shooting stars are shot at the *Shayateen* on that night. It lasts until the break of the dawn (the start of fajr). Another sign is that the sun rises without any very beams beams of light, appearing rather like the moon in its fullness. On that day, Allah ﷻ stops the *Shayateen* from rising up with the sun."

Note: Part of what has been stated in this *Hadeeth* has already been discussed. Some signs are here related about the actual night. These signs are clear and need no further explanation. Apart from these, there are other signs too, as stated in the *Ahaadeeth* or in the experiences of those who had the good fortune to experience *Laylatul Qadr.*

The sign that is, however, most specific in the *Hadeeth* is the rising of the sun, without any very bright beams of light. Other signs are not always found. A *Sahaabi,* Abdah bin Abi Lubaaba ؓ says: "On the evening of the 27th, I tasted the water of the sea and it was sweet." Ayyoob Ibn Khalid said: "I once had to bath myself with sea water and on tasting it, found it sweet. This was on the 23rd night."

Some of the pious people have written that on the evening of *Laylatul Qadr*, everything goes into *sajdah* before Allah ﷻ, so much so that trees fall flat on the ground and then return to their normal position. However, these are such signs which cannot be seen by the ordinary person.

What dua a person should make on Laylatul Qadr

Aa'isha رضي الله عنها reports, "I said 'O Rasul of Allah ﷻ , should I find myself in *Laylatul Qadr*, what shall I ask of Allah ﷻ ?'" Rasulullah ﷺ replied, "Say, 'O Allah, You are the One who grants pardon for sins, You love to pardon, so pardon me.'" (Reported by Ahmad, Ibn Majah and Tirmidhi)

Note: This is such an all-inclusive *dua*, where we beg that Allah ﷻ in His kindness should forgive our sins. If we get forgiven, what more do we need? Imaam Sufyan al-Thawree رَحْمَةُ اللهِ عَلَيْه use to say that to remain busy on this night with *dua* is better than any other form of worship of Allah ﷻ.

Ibn Rajab رَحْمَةُ اللهِ عَلَيْه says that we should not only remain busy with *dua* but should also take part in all other forms of worship of Allah ﷻ, e.g. recitation of the Qur'aan, *Salaah,* meditation etc. This opinion is most correct and nearer to what Rasulullah ﷺ has said, as already stated in the previous *Ahaadeeth.*

I'itikaaf (Staying in the Musjid)

Hadeeth no. 1

Abu Sa'iyd Khudri رضي الله عنه reports that Rasulullah ﷺ once performed *i'itikaaf* for the first ten days of Ramadhaan. Thereafter, he made *i'itikaaf* in a Turkish tent (inside the *Musjid*) for the middle ten days. Thereafter, he raised his head out of the tent and said, "Verily, in search of *Laylatul Qadr* did I perform *i'itikaaf* for the first ten days, then for the middle ten days. Then someone (an angel) came and told me, 'It is in the last ten days. Whosoever has made *i'itikaaf* with me should continue for the last ten days.' I had been shown that night and then made to forget, which it how it shall be. I saw myself making *sajda* to Allah تعالى with my forehead on mud the next morning. Look for *Laylatul Qadr* in the last ten nights of Ramadhaan; look for it among the odd nights."

Abu Sa'iyd رضي الله عنه says; "That same night it rained. The roof on the *Musjid* leaked. I looked at Rasulullah ﷺ eyes and forehead and there were remains of water and mud. This was on the morning of the 21st after performing *sujood* in muddy clay". (Reported in Mishkaat)

Commentary

It used to be the general practice of Rasulullah ﷺ to perform *i'itikaaf* in Ramadhaan. At times he used to remain in the *Musjid* for the whole month and during the last year of his life he was in *i'itikaaf* for twenty days. Because he always stayed in the *Musjid* for last ten days, the *Ulama'* say that it *sunnah-e-mu'akkadah* to perform *i'itikaaf* in last ten days.

From the above *Hadeeth* it can be understood that the main object of *i'itikaaf* was to search for *Laylatul Qadr*. What better way of searching can there be than to be in *i'itikaaf*, because we are considered to be in *ibaadah* all the time, whether we are awake or asleep.

Furthermore, one in *i'itikaaf* is free from all daily works and thus has all the time to spend in *zikrullah*, (the remembrance of Allah ﷻ) and meditation. Throughout Ramadhaan, Rasulullah ﷺ worked very hard at increased his *ibaadah* and when the last ten days came along, he had no limit in pushing himself. He himself remained awake throughout the night and awakened his family for the same purpose.

Aa'isha رضي الله عنها reports: "During Ramadhaan, Rasullullah ﷺ tied his *lungi* tightly about him, staying awake all night and waking his family (for the purpose of *ibaadah*)." 'Tied his *lungi* tightly means that he spent all his time in *ibaadah*.

Hadeeth no. 2

Ibn Abbas ؓ relates that Rasullullah ﷺ said, "The person performing *i'itikaaf* remains free from sins, and he is given the same reward as those who do good deeds in spite of not having done those deeds because of staying in the *Musjid*." (Reported in Mishkaat from ibn Majah)

Commentary

One in *i'itikaaf* in the *Musjid* is not allowed to leave for his worldly needs. He may only come out use the toilet or to perform *wudhu* or *ghusl* or for attending *Jumuah* when that is not performed in that *Musjid*, after which he must return immediately. This *Hadeeth* teaches us two great benefits of *i'itikaaf.*

Firstly we are saved from sin. It is true that many times we commit sins without intending to do so. (The world all around us is full of temptations). To commit sin in the blessed month of Ramadhaan is a great harm to ourselves. By remaining in the *Musjid*, we completely avoid the temptation to commit sin. Secondly, it would seem that when we are in *i'itikaaf* in the *Musjid*, we are automatically at a disadvantage by not being allowed to perform certain good deeds like joining funeral prayers, attending burials, visiting the sick, etc. That is not so, because according to this *Hadeeth*, we are rewarded for these actions even though we did not perform them. What a great favour from Allah ﷻ! How great is Allah's ﷻ bounty! By performing our *ibaadah*, we receive the reward of many other *ibaadaat*. In fact, Allah ﷻ looks for the smallest excuse to give us His blessings. His blessings could be received plentifully with a little effort and asking. If only we can understand and properly appreciate these favours. That proper appreciation and understanding can only enter our minds when we have the true love and interest for our *Deen*. May Allah ﷻ grant us that. *Aameen*

The Last Night of Ramadhaan

Ibn Abbaas ؓ says that, he heard our Nabi ﷺ saying, "*Jannah* becomes perfumed with the sweetest fragrance in Ramadhaan. From the beginning of the year till the end, it is being brightly decorated for this blessed month. When the first night of Ramadhaan appears, a wind blows from beneath the *Arsh* (Throne). It is called *Mutheerah*, which causes the leaves of the trees of *Jannah* to rustle and door handles to sound, causing such a beautiful sound as had never been heard before. The dark eyed beautiful ladies of *Jannah* then step forward till they appear in the centre of the balconies of *Jannah*, saying: 'Is there anyone making *dua* to Allah ﷻ for us that Allah ﷻ may marry us to him?' Then these women call out: 'O Ridhwaan, keeper of Jannah, what night is this?' He replies: '*labbaik*, this is the first night of Ramadhaan, when the doors of *Jannah* are opened to those who keep the fast from among the *ummah* of Muhammad ﷺ.'"

Rasulullah ﷺ further said, Allah ﷻ says, "O Ridhwaan open the doors of *Jannah*, and O Maalik, (keeper of Jahannam) close the doors of *Jahannam* for those who fast from the *ummah* of Ahmad ﷺ (another name for Nabi ﷺ), O Jibraeel go down to the earth and tie the evil *Shayaateen*, put them in chains and throw them in the oceans so that they make no mischief, thereby spoiling the fast of the *ummah* of My beloved Muhammad ﷺ."

Allah ﷻ commands a caller from the heavens to call out three times on every one of the nights of Ramadhaan: "Is there anyone begging of Me that I may grant him his desire? Is there anyone repenting to me that I may turn in mercy to him? Is there anyone begging for forgiveness that I may forgive him? Who is there who shall give a loan to the One whose wealth does not become less and the One who fulfils without cutting short unjustly?"

Rasulullah ﷺ then said, "Every day at the time of *iftaar*, Allah ﷻ sets free one million people from the fire of *Jahannam*, all of whom had already earned entrance into *Jahannam.* On the last night He sets free as many as had been set free throughout the month. On the night of *Laylatul Qadr*, Allah ﷻ commands Jibraeel عليه السلام to go down to the earth with a group of *Malaaikah* (Angels). They go down carrying a green flag which is then planted on top of the Kabah. Jibraeel عليه السلام himself has one hundred wings, only two of which are spread out on this night. He spreads out these wings which cover from the east to the west. Jibraeel عليه السلام then sends out the *Malaaikah* on this night in all directions to recite salaam upon each and everyone they find in *ibaadah* (prayer) or sitting, performing *Salaah* and praising Allah ﷻ. They shake hands with them and say '*Aameen*' to all their *duas* until dawn. When dawn comes, Jibraeel عليه السلام calls out; 'depart O *Malaaikah* of Allah depart.'"

The *Malaaikah* then inquire: "O Jibraeel, but what did Allah ﷻ do regarding the needs of the faithful people from among the *ummah* of Ahmad ﷺ which they asked from Him?"

Jibraeel عليه السلام replies: "Allah ﷻ looked at them with mercy and forgave them all except four kinds of people."

Then we the *Sahaabah* رضي الله عنهم asked: "Who are they, O Rasulullah ﷺ?"

Rasulullah ﷺ replied, "They are the people who drink wine, those disobedient to their parents, those who do not speak to their near relatives and the *mushaahin.*"

We asked, "O Rasulullah ﷺ who is a *mushaahin*?"

He replied: "Those who have bad feelings in their hearts for their brothers and break off relations with them".

The night of *Eidul Fitr*, the night that is called *Laylatul Jaa'izah* (The night of prize giving), comes along. On the morning of *Eid*, Allah ﷻ sends down the *Malaaikah*, to all the lands of the earth, where they stand at the entrance of roads, calling out with a voice that is heard by all except man and jinn: "O *Ummah* of Muhammad ﷺ, come out of your houses towards a Lord that is noble and gracious, who grants much and pardons the big sins."

When they go towards the places for their *Eid Salaah*, Allah ﷻ says to the *Malaaikah*: "What is the reward of that worker who has completed his work?"

The *Malaaikah* reply: "O Lord and master, it is only right that he should receive his reward in full."

Allah ﷻ then says: "I call you to witness, O My *Malaaikah*, that for their having fasted during the month of Ramadhaan, and for their having stood before Me in prayer by night, I have granted to them as reward My pleasure and have granted them forgiveness. O My servants ask now of Me, for I swear by My honour and My greatness, that whatsoever you shall beg of Me this day in this gathering of yours for the needs of the Hereafter, I shall grant you, and whatsoever you shall ask for your worldly needs, I shall grant it. I swear by My honour that, as long as you shall obey My commands, I shall cover up your faults. By My Honour and My Greatness do I swear that I shall never disgrace you together with the sinful people and disbelievers. Go now from here, you are forgiven. You have pleased Me and I am pleased with you."

The *Malaaikah* on seeing this great reward given by Allah ﷻ upon the *ummah* of Muhammad ﷺ on the day of *Eidul Fitr* become greatly pleased and happy. (As reported in Targheeb.)

"O Allah ﷻ, make us also of those lucky ones, *Aameen.*"

Commentary

The previous pages of this book already covered almost all that is contained in this last long *Hadeeth.* A few points need attention. We see here that there are a few people who do not get forgiven in Ramadhaan and are very unlucky in not being able to share the great gifts of Allah ﷻ on the morning of *Eid.* Among them are those who fight and argue amongst themselves and those disobedient to their parents. Let us ask those people one question: "You have displeased Allah ﷻ and having done so, what other place can you go to besides Allah ﷻ?" We feel very sad that for some reason or the other you have made yourselves the target for the curse of Allah ﷻ, His Rasul ﷺ and Jibraeel عليه السلام while at the same time you have been left out from Allah's ﷻ forgiveness which is freely granted.

Who else can grant you safety? Who and what can stand by your side when you carry the curse of Rasulullah ﷺ? Who can help you when Allah's ﷻ close angel Jibraeel عليه السلام has made *dua* against you? While Allah ﷻ is excluding you from His forgiveness and mercy, I beg you my dear brother and sister to think about your position at this moment. Think and give up all that which takes you away from Allah ﷻ. There is time to change and repent and now is that time. To-morrow you shall have to stand before a Judge before whom no rank, honour, position and wealth shall help you. A Judge before whom only actions shall count and Who is always aware of our every movement. Remember that Allah ﷻ may forgive our faults as far as our relationship with Him is concerned, but will not forgive, without punishment, our mistakes in our relations with other people.

Rasulullah ﷺ said: "The bankrupt one from among my *ummah* is that person, who shall appear on the day of *Qiyaamah*, bringing with him good actions like *Salaah*, *Sawm* (fast) and charity, however, he had also sworn at someone, falsely accused someone else and hurt someone, with the result that all these people shall come forward with their complaints against him, giving witness against him. As a penalty, his good deeds shall be taken away and granted to the wronged ones. When his good deeds shall come to an end, then the wronged persons sins shall be thrown upon him (when he is not able to pay the full penalty because of not having enough good deeds). Hence, in this way he shall enter *Jahannam*." We see that in spite of many good deeds, his state of regret and sorry cannot be described. (O Allah! save us from that).

Many times we have read about so many occasions and actions which become the reason for our forgiveness. The question now comes about that when forgiveness is being granted why should it be granted time and again? In other words, once a person had been forgiven there are no sins left on him. So why is forgiveness granted again? The answer is that, when forgiveness comes to a person with sins on him, it will mean those sins are wiped off, but when he has no sin, it will mean that mercy and favour is granted to him.

Another interesting point to note is that Allah ﷻ time and again calls the *Malaaikah* to witness. The question may come about that why is it so? Here we should remember that the court of *Qiyaamah* for reckoning is ready, so that witnesses shall be brought forward to testify. Hence *Ambiyaa* عليهم السلام shall be required to bring witnesses as to whether they had delivered the message. Very often our Nabi ﷺ used to say, "You shall be asked about me (and my mission). So bear witness that I did deliver the message."

The last *Hadeeth* also gives a joyous message to the lucky ones. Allah ﷻ says that He shall not disgrace and humiliate those who did their duties in front of (and among) the unbelievers and evil doers. This is the greatness of Allah's ﷻ grace and kindness and also the importance Allah ﷻ shows for the position of the Muslims. In addition for those who wanted Allah's ﷻ pleasure, another of His blessing and favour is that their faults and sins will also be covered.

Abdullah ibnu Umar رضي الله عنه reports that Rasulullah ﷺ said, "On the day of *Qiyaamah*, Allah ﷻ shall call a muslim to come near to Him. A curtain shall be closed so that none may see. Allah ﷻ shall then remind him of each and every fault of his which he shall be forced to admit. Seeing the great amount of his faults, that person shall feel that he had certainly failed and shall be destroyed. But then Allah ﷻ will say: 'In the world I covered your faults and today too I will hide them and forgive them for you.'" Thereafter his book of good deeds shall be given to him.

The meaning of this *Hadeeth* is contained in many other *Ahaadeeth* as well. We should therefore be careful of not humiliating and attacking the pious people for their faults, because it is possible that their faults are forgiven. It is also possible that we may be the real losers through backbiting and teasing those who in their own way are trying to please Allah ﷻ. It is possible that Allah ﷻ may cover their faults and forgive them through the blessings of their other good actions, while we who continue to backbite, laugh and mock them, may be the cause of our own destruction. (May Allah ﷻ in His Mercy pardon us all).

This *Hadeeth* also states that the night before the day of *Eid* is called the night of prize giving, the night when Allah ﷻ gives the true reward. This night too should be properly appreciated. Usually, once the announcement has been made that tomorrow is *Eid*, most of us, even the pious, enjoy ourselves in sleep on this night, whereas this too is a night that should be spent in *ibaadah*.

Rasulullah ﷺ said, "Whoever remains awake for *ibaadah* on the nights before both *Eids* with the aim of gaining reward, his heart shall not die on that day when hearts shall die." The meaning here is that at the time when evil will overpower all, his heart shall stay alive (guarded against evil). It may also refer to the time when the horn shall be blown to announce the day of *Qiyaamah.* On that day he will not become unconscious.

Rasulullah ﷺ is also reported to have said, "Whoever stays awake for *ibaadah* on the following five nights, entrance into *Jannah* becomes *waajib* for him, *Laylatul Tarwiyah* (the night before the eight Zil Hijjah), *Laylatul Arafah* (the night before the ninth Zul Hijjah), *Laylatul Nahr* (the night before the tenth Zul Hijjah), the night before *Eidul Fitr* and the night before the fifteenth of Shabaan.

The *Ulama'* have written that it is *mustahab* to remain in *ibaadah* on the nights before *Eid.* It is reported by Imaam Shafi رَحْمَةُ اللهِ عَلَيْهِ that, there are five nights in which *duas* are accepted; The night preceding Friday, the night before both *Eids*, the first night of Rajab and *Laylatul Baraa'h* (the fifteenth of Shabaan).

Among the pious in Islaam it is said that, because of the exceptional greatness of Friday night, we should spend this night in *ibaadah* during the month of Ramadhaan. However, there are some *Ahaadeeth* where we have been stopped from fixing only that night for *ibaadah.* It is best that one or two other nights should be joined with it.

I have now come to the end of this book. In conclusion, hoping that this shall be of benefit to those who look for Allah's ﷻ pleasure, I beg all readers to make *dua* for me, the humble writer of these pages, during those special hours of Ramadhaan. It is possible that because of your *duas*, Allah ﷻ bestows His happiness and love upon me too. *Aameen.*

www.ingramcontent.com/pod-product-compliance
Lightning Source LLC
Chambersburg PA
CBHW062202160726
48282CB00027B/961
* 9 7 8 8 1 1 9 0 2 4 2 1 6 *